TEQUILA MOCKINGBIRD

MINI BOOK

TIM FEDERLE

T0364018

A Running Press® Miniature Edition™
© 2017 by Tim Federle
Illustrations © 2017 by Lauren Mortimer

Adapted from *Tequila Mockingbird: Cocktails with a Literary Twist*,
published in 2013 by Running Press.

ISBN 978-0-7624-6154-7

Published by Running Press Book Publishers,
An Imprint of Perseus Books, LLC.,
A Subsidiary of Hachette Book Group, Inc.
2300 Chestnut Street
Philadelphia, PA 19103-4371

www.runningpress.com

Introduction

Gentle Drinker:

Congrats. You fought through *War and Peace*, burned through *Fahrenheit 451*, and sailed through *Moby-Dick*—and you deserve a drink! Hang tight, undergrad. A beer's not going to cut it. Not this time.

To pay homage to the world's greatest stories and storytellers, we've curated this perfectly portable kit full of literature-inspired cocktails. Scholarly sips for word nerds, if you will. Welcome to *The Tequila Mockingbird Kit*.

So grab a glass. Let's get a little stupid and look a little smart. Even if you don't have a BA in English, tonight you're gonna drink like you do.

Glassware and Equipment

Cocktail (or martini) glass (4 to 6 ounces): Drinks are shaken and strained into this long-stemmed, iconic v-shaped beauty.

Collins glass (10 to 14 ounces): Built like a highball glass, but taller and narrower. Best for icy, very large tropical drinks. Also best for getting drunk.

Flute (4 to 6 ounces): Champagne cocktails are served in this specially designed stemware, which showcases the bubbles without letting too many of them fly free.

Highball glass (10 to 12 ounces):
Midway between a rocks and a Collins glass. If you could only have one glass in your arsenal, it should be this.

Rocks (or lowball or old-fashioned) glass (6 to 10 ounces): A drink poured "on the rocks"—that's over ice, rookie—is frequently served in one of these short, heavy tumblers.

Shot glass (¾ to 2 ounces): For ~~slamming back~~ calmly enjoying a variety of aptly named "shots." The smallest of drinking vessels, these are also handy as measuring devices.

Pitcher and punch bowl: Best for serving all the nonfiction characters in your life. Half-gallon pitchers and gallon punch bowls do the trick.

Shaker: An essential device that need not intimidate! Our fave is the Cobbler: a three-part metal contraption (counting the capped lid) with the strainer built right in.

Jigger: For small liquid measurements. A metal hourglass shape, available in a variety of sizes. Conveniently for you, we've included a fancy jigger in this very kit. The larger side holds 1 ounce and the smaller side holds ½ ounce.

TEQUILA MOCKINGBIRD

To Kill a Mockingbird (1960)
By Harper Lee

Little Scout Finch narrates this oft-taught tale, in which an Alabama town rallies behind a lying drunk's lying daughter, who's up and accused an innocent African-American man of taking advantage of her. Lucky for Scout—who watches from a courtroom balcony as her lawyer father defends the man—she's got levelheaded pals by her side. After a conclusion that leaves you both hopeful and haunted, toast to a sometimes sour justice system with this feisty tequila shot.

1 ½ ounces tequila

2 drops hot sauce

1 Dill (get it?) pickle

....

Pour the tequila into a shot glass, add the hot sauce, and slam that bad boy back before chasing with a big chomp of pickle. No tears allowed here: if you can't stand the heat, get out of the South.

TEQUILA MOCKINGBIRD

A COCKTAIL OF TWO CITIES

A Tale of Two Cities (1859)
By Charles Dickens

Though Paris and London are the real stars in this Dickens classic, there's also a tragically romantic love story that plays out on their streets, starring a golden-haired beauty and the two men who are willing to die for her (talk about "the best of times"). Toast to sooty chivalry with our take on a famous drink that hails from "The New York Bar" in Paris.

1 sugar cube

1 ounce gin

½ ounce lemon juice

Champagne, to fill

....

Place the sugar cube in a flute. Pour the gin and lemon juice into a shaker with ice, and shake well. Strain into the flute. Fill to the top with Champagne. The result is revolutionary.

A COCKTAIL OF TWO CITIES

CRIME AND PUNISH-MINT

Crime and Punishment (1866)
By Fyodor Dostoyevsky

New readers of *Crime and Punishment*—the tortured tale of a man who feels destined to murder a pawnbroker and then redistribute the wealth—might think they're tuning in for a literary *Law & Order*. Those readers are wrong. Forget primetime courtroom scenes, because the only punishment here is the murderer's life sentence of guilt. Pair Russia's homeland brew—vodka, baby!—with just enough caffeine to give you the shakes. The mint should calm your nerves before you do anything too crazy.

1½ ounces vodka

½ ounce coffee liqueur

½ ounce crème de menthe liqueur

Light cream, to fill

....

Pour the vodka and liqueurs over ice in a rocks glass. Fill to the top with light cream—or heavy. Hey, you only live once.

CRIME AND PUNISH-MINT

ONE FLEW OVER THE COSMO'S NEST

One Flew Over the Cuckoo's Nest (1962)
By Ken Kesey

Though narrated by a paranoid side-character, the hero of Kesey's groundbreaking novel is McMurphy, who leads his fellow mental patients in a rebellion against Nurse Ratched, a needlewielding vixen who represents the tyranny of society—and raises the question "Who's the real crazy here?" Liberate your own hemmed-in ways with a Cosmo you'd be cuckoo to pass on.

1½ ounces vodka

1 ounce cranberry juice

½ ounce triple sec

½ ounce lime juice

....

Combine the ingredients with ice in a shaker. Shake well and strain into a chilled cocktail glass. Code blue: it's hard to stop at just one of these— especially if all the other voices in your head are parched, too.

ONE FLEW OVER THE COSMO'S NEST

DRANKENSTEIN

Frankenstein (1818)
By Mary Shelley

Mary Shelley created more than a monster when she anonymously published *Frankenstein* at age twenty-one—she also birthed one of pop culture's greatest misattributions: Frankenstein is the name of the whacko doctor, not the green-faced, peg-necked creature. Try your own experiment with the following Halloween-ready, bright green concoction.

1 ounce melon liqueur

1 ounce tequila

1 (12-ounce) can club soda

....

Pour the liqueur and tequila over ice in a highball glass, then fill to the top with the club soda. Now, light a few candles, lock the door, and guard your potion with monosyllabic grunts.

DRANKENSTEIN

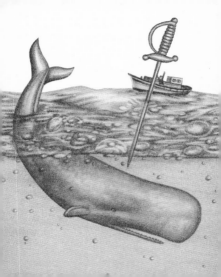

MOBY-DRINK

Moby-Dick (1851)
By Herman Melville

In Melville's *Moby-Dick*, published first in England (and greeted with scathing reviews!), the titular whale is best known for attacking Captain Ahab's ship and then chewing off the poor fella's leg. Ahab spends the rest of his career limping around, determined to exact revenge on Moby-D, only to finally spear the whale and—Plan B!—get dragged underwater to his own ironic death. Grab a harpoon (swizzle stick) and get even (drunk).

1 ounce vodka

½ ounce Blue Curaçao

1 (12-ounce) can lemon-lime soda

1 Swedish Fish candy, for garnish

....

Combine the vodka and Blue Curaçao over ice in a highball glass and fill to the top with the lemon-lime soda. Now for the demonic part: grab that Swedish Fish by the gills, spear it with a swizzle stick, and get plunging. Just don't fall in yourself.

MOBY-DRINK

ROMEO AND JULEP

Romeo and Juliet (Circa 1599)
By William Shakespeare

This melancholy romance is for anyone who has fallen in love with the hot boy from the other side of the tracks. Who can't relate to the star-crossed lovers, doomed from the start by parents who, like, just don't understand? With a tragic, poisonous finale, this historic work created the mold, inspiring countless adaptations. Fall under the spell of a drink so spring-like and peach-fuzzy, you might be forgiven for not realizing its full effects.

6 sprigs fresh mint, washed

1 teaspoon light brown sugar

½ ounce peach schnapps

1½ ounces bourbon

1 (12-ounce) can lemon-lime soda

In a highball glass, muddle the mint, sugar, and schnapps until the sugar dissolves like a relationship over summer break. Add ice and bourbon, and fill to the top with the lemon-lime soda.

ROMEO AND JULEP

LORD OF THE MAI-TAIS

Lord of the Flies (1954)
By William Golding

If you went to a high school that favored broadened minds over banned books, you'll remember devouring this fable of order and disorder, schoolboys–turned–savages, and one very trippy pig's head. Recommended reading during your next flight to Hawaii, escape to the galley if things get bumpy and throw together this Polynesian nerve-calmer.

2 ounces cranberry juice

2 ounces orange juice

1½ ounces light rum

1 ounce coconut rum

1 teaspoon grenadine syrup

Orange slice or pineapple wedge, for garnish (optional)

....

Shake the ingredients with ice—odds are, it'll all turn out bloody red—and pour everything, including the ice, into a Collins glass. Get creative with the tropical garnishes: pineapples, oranges, eye of piglet. . .

LORD OF THE MAI-TAIS

INFINITE ZEST

Infinite Jest (1996)
By David Foster Wallace

Cofounding and delightful in equal measure, this rule-breaking modern classic is infamous for sprawling prose, endless footnotes,[1] and a madcap depiction of the future.[2] *Jest* takes place in the 'burbs of Boston, between a halfway house and a nearby tennis academy. Serve up a tennis-ball-yellow cocktail that mimics the zest and bounce of Wallace's magnum opus.

[1] Just like this, they appeared at the end of the book—over four hundred of 'em!

[2] Time is marked with corporate sponsorships, as in Year of the Perdue Wonderchicken.

2 ounces vodka

1 ounce limoncello

½ ounce lemon juice

....

Minding that tennis elbow, shake the ingredients with ice and strain into a cocktail glass. Head back to the court, sport, and never give up on your game.

INFINITE ZEST

THE LIME OF THE
ANCIENT MARINER

The Rime of the Ancient Mariner (1798)
By Samuel Taylor Coleridge

Next time you're marooned on an island,
resist the temptation to call out, "Water,
water everywhere, and not a drop to
drink!" The actual phrase—"Water, water
everywhere, nor any drop to drink"—is
from an epic poem about bad weather,
angry oceans, and pissed-off dead birds
who aren't afraid to haunt a hull. Celebrate
your land legs with this limey twist on a
salty classic.

Sea salt, for highball rim

2 ounces lime juice

2 ounces grapefruit juice

1½ ounces gin

....

Rim a chilled highball glass in sea salt. Fill the glass with ice, pour in the ingredients, and give a good stir. When you're sobered up, matey, head back to the lookout deck— and watch out for low-flying birds.

THE LIME OF THE ANCIENT MARINER

ORANGE JULIUS CAESAR

Julius Caesar (Circa 1599)
By William Shakespeare

With pals like this, who needs enemies? Shakespeare's *Julius Caesar* reads like a luxuriantly extended definition of the word "backstabber," as the title character's rise in power inspires those closest to him to plot his assassination. Though Caesar gets top billing, he actually appears in only a handful of scenes; the real star here is Marcus Brutus. Sneak a little mother's milk into an old-fashioned breakfast recipe—and trust us (no, really, you can trust us), the result is pretty killer.

3 ounces orange juice

2 ounces milk

1½ ounces light rum

1 teaspoon granulated sugar

¼ teaspoon vanilla

··

Have your closest frenemy load all the ingredients, plus a handful of ice, into your blender. Only after he removes his fingers, get whirring. Serve in a Collins glass.

ORANGE JULIUS CAESAR

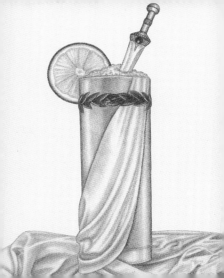

THE OLD MAN AND THE SEAGRAM'S

The Old Man and the Sea (1952)
By Ernest Hemingway

A Pulitzer winner drowning in biblical allegory, *The Old Man and the Sea* was Hemingway's final published work in a career dripping with awards and accolades—and alcohol. The premise is simple: an old man sets out to destroy a fish in an act of single-minded delirium. During an epic three-day battle in which the marlin is finally defeated, hitched to the side of the boat, and eaten by sharks en route to shore, the old man emerges weary but victorious. Do your best sailor imitation with the standby gear of any fisherman: whiskey and bait.

2 ounces whiskey (like Seagram's)

1 (12-ounce) can lemon-lime soda

Kumquat, for garnish

Combine the whiskey and lemon-lime soda over ice in a highball glass. Grab some fishing tackle (looks like a fish; has a hook), give it a soapy scrubbing, and then bait 'n' float your kumquat. Just don't sip and sail.

THE OLD MAN AND THE SEAGRAM'S

THE LAST OF THE MOJITOS

The Last of the Mohicans (1826)
By James Fenimore Cooper

Long before the universally adored film came out, *The Last of the Mohicans* was landmark (if historically wobbly) literature. Chronicling the tomahawk-assisted turf wars of Native Americans, Cooper stuffed his pages with wordy, witless plot-stoppers—but we'll help you through the slow parts. Take a classic *mojito* and launch your own sneak attack, losing the sugar for agave nectar and adding a few authentically Native American fruits to the party. The result could stop wars.

5 fresh blueberries, washed

3 small, fresh strawberries, washed

8 sprigs fresh mint, washed

½ ounce lemon juice

1 ounce agave nectar

1½ ounces light rum

1 (12-ounce) can club soda

....

Muddle the berries, mint, juice, and nectar in a Collins glass. Add two handfuls ice and the rum, give a good stir, and top off with the club soda. Expect a rain dance of happy tears.

THE LAST OF THE MOJITOS

FAHRENHEIT 151

Fahrenheit 451 (1953)
By Ray Bradbury

Bradbury's then-futuristic *Fahrenheit 451* (the temperature at which a book burns) is about a truly unthinkable society in which technology reigns supreme and books go bye-bye. Written in the fifties but ringing eerily true today, Fahrenheit's world stars firemen who start the flames, setting the written word afire and sniffing out pesky, law-breaking readers. Serve up a burning-hot party drink to toast the peerless printed page—hey, you don't wanna spill rum on a Kindle.

Makes about 10 drinks

6 cups apple cider

1 cup cranberry juice

1 cup orange juice

1 cup pineapple juice

6 cloves

4 cinnamon sticks

8 ounces rum (like Bacardi 151)

....

Pour the ingredients, except the rum, into a crock pot. Warm for approximately 1 hour, or until heated through. Unplug the pot and add the rum. Give it a stir and ladle away.

FAHRENHEIT 151

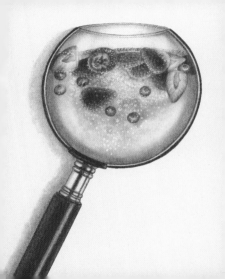

THE ADVENTURES OF SHERBET HOLMES

The Adventures of Sherlock Holmes
(1891–92)
By Sir Arthur Conan Doyle

Here's an ode to one of Conan Doyle's lesserknown stories from his blazingly popular magazine series: "The Blue Carbuncle," a Holmes whodunit involving a goose with a very expensive gem lodged very inconveniently in its neck. After you trade jewels for berries, the only remaining mystery will be why you've never made this party pleaser before.

Makes about 10 drinks

1 quart berry sherbet

1 bottle (about 3 cups) Champagne,
chilled

1 liter ginger ale

½ cup fresh blueberries,
washed, for garnish

....

Empty the sherbet into a punch bowl
and pour the Champagne and ginger
ale on top. Float the blueberries and
serve. Don't leave the room for long—
you'll return to a fast-empty bowl and
a classic whodrunkit.

**THE ADVENTURES OF
SHERBET HOLMES**

For more literary cocktails, check out Tim Federle's full-length *Tequila Mockingbird* ($15, Running Press).

This book has been bound using handcraft methods and Smyth-sewn to ensure durability.

The text was written by Tim Federle.

The text was abridged and edited by Jessica Fromm.

Illustrations by Lauren Mortimer.

Designed by Joshua McDonnell.

The text was set in Bembo, Copperplate, and Phosphorus.